W9-ANJ-272

PLAIN PRAYERS FOR A COMPLICATED WORLD

PLAIN PRAYERS FOR A COMPLICATED WORLD

by AVERY BROOKE

Illustrated by RONALD KURILOFF

READER'S DIGEST PRESS

Distributed by Thomas Y. Crowell Company,
New York, 1975

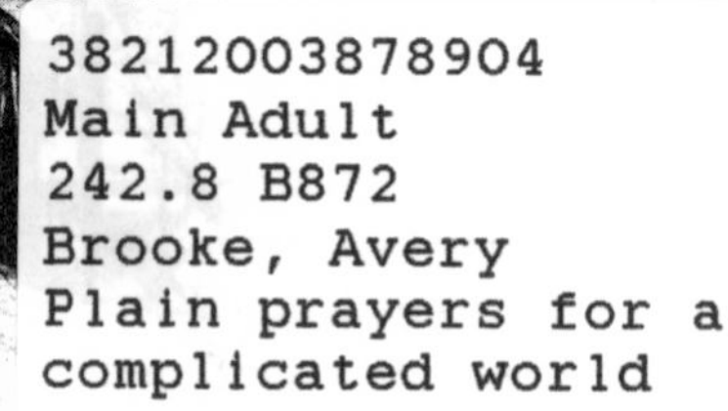

 Published simultaneously in Canada by Fitzhenry & Whiteside, Limited, Toronto.

Manufactured in the United States of America.

Library of Congress Catalogue Card No.: 75-10614

ISBN: 0-88349-060-9
0-88349-061-9 (paper)

Library of Congress Cataloging in Publication Data

Brooke, Avery.
Plain prayers for a complicated world.

1. Prayers. I. Title.
BV245.B673 242'.8 75-10614
ISBN 0-88349-060-9
ISBN 0-88349-061-9 pbk.

CONTENTS

FOR
Marian Taylor

PREFACE

YEARS AGO I wrote a book of everyday prayers for young people. To my surprise the most common adult response was "But this is not just for children, it's for me."

I should not have been surprised, for I have always believed that whatever the differences in age and personality and whatever the particularities of circumstance, the true words of one human being spoken to God find echoes in the hearts of the rest of us. Essentially we are not all that different. The joy and pain felt at eight has a great deal in common with the joy and pain felt at eighty. When, therefore, I was urged to write a book that would be *designed* for people of any age, I was challenged.

As I look over the prayers I wrote years ago and the ones I have written more recently, I find two marked differences: The newer prayers often have a deeper honesty. I could not have written "The Difficulty of Loving" fifteen years ago. Also, as we grow older, our experience broadens and there are more things to pray about. Our prayers are just as plain—indeed sometimes plainer—but our world, both inner and outer, has become more complicated. Many books of prayers in everyday words are available today, and a number are excellent, but for the most part they are not only *by* individuals but *for* individuals—something to be read and pondered in solitude. It is my hope that this book, while it may be read in solitude, may also be shared, that parent and child, grandparent and grandchild, friend and friend may wish to share these prayers and through them discover the existence of deeper common bonds than they had realized they possessed.

Avery Brooke

PLAIN PRAYERS FOR A COMPLICATED WORLD

HOW LARGE IS YOUR LOVE

O LORD, how large is your love!
My heart sings to you and the stones beneath my feet and the sky above my head sing also. All around me is your world and I know that you know all of it and it knows your love. My thoughts leap at the wonder of it. It is all yours, from the little stones at my feet to the unending sky above.

O Lord, such a great knowing you have beyond counting and such a great loving beyond measure! And I am caught up in it and sing of it to the world and to you.

A MORNING PRAYER

TAKE my hand, Lord, and lead me through this day, step by step. Remind me that I cannot do everything I wish, nor do any of it perfectly. Only you are perfect, and only with your help can I do my best. Help me to remember to ask for that help.

AN EVENING PRAYER

FATHER, I have much to be grateful for tonight, and I thank you. I have much to regret and I ask your forgiveness. But even as I ask your forgiveness I know that I receive it, and a deep peace fills my heart.

Help me to sleep well tonight and to wake ready for that daily yet greatest of gifts, a fresh start.

TO PRAY FOR STRANGERS

GOD, when I am in need, or those I know and love are in need, it is easy to ask for your help. But it is more difficult to pray for strangers. Even when I know they are in great trouble, their needs seem very distant. Help me to imagine how they feel so that I may pray for them, not just with words but with my heart.

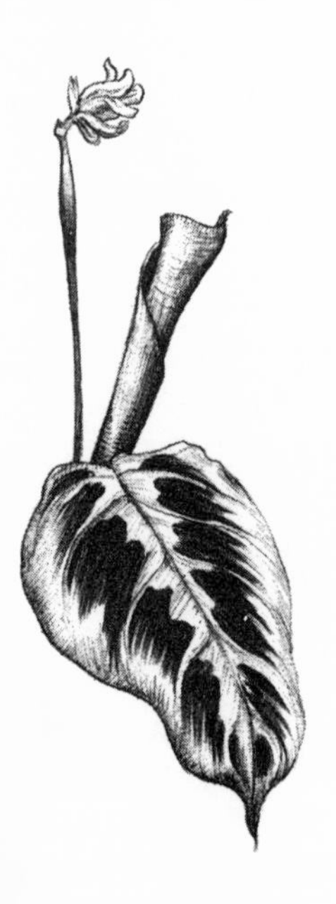

THE DIFFICULTY OF LOVING

GOD, you tell us to love. To love people and to love you.

Sometimes it is easy. The whole world seems to sing and we look at strangers and those close to us and our hearts smile. But it isn't always easy. Even—or particularly—with those closest to us. Where words said or unsaid mean so much more, where needs cry out and hurts go deep, there is more chance for things to get all tangled. We mean too much to each other and we cannot express it.

O Christ, help us to see clearly when nothing is clear, to speak in love when feeling unloved, and to have the wisdom and patience to speak the right words at the right time.

To try

THERE are countless things to do in this world of yours, and I know that I don't have to try to do them all. But there are some things that I should do.

If I am not very good at something it is so easy to forget about it, or to say that I don't like it, or just not try very hard.

Help me to try, God, to try without holding back and without fear of failure. And when I do fail, grant me the courage to try again with a light and cheerful heart.

Good and Bad Fortune

Help me to be thankful, God, for all the good things in my life and not take them for granted. And when things go wrong, help me not to be too sorry for myself but to remember so many other people whose lives are much harder: people who are always hungry, who are sick with no one to care for them, who have ability but no chance to learn. Help me to pray for them and forget myself.

LIKING AND BEING LIKED

SOMETIMES I get so caught up in worrying about whether people like me that I don't stop to think about my liking them. I know that's backward, God, but it's so hard to remember.

Help me to forget what others think of me and lose myself in getting to know them, enjoy them and love them.

I FEEL ANGRY AND HURT

EVERYTHING seemed fine, God. I did the very best I could and I felt happy about it. But no one cares and I feel angry and hurt.

I think that they have been unfair to me. Perhaps they have, God, and perhaps they haven't, but in either case I need to understand. Help me to think clearly, to act wisely and not to hold a grudge.

THE WORLD IS BEFORE ME

O CHRIST, the world is before me and I could do many things. Help me to choose wisely where I should go and what I should do.

Sometimes I dream prideful dreams of being very important and having everyone look up to me, and other times I think I can't really do much of anything.

Help me to dream, Christ, but to dream good and possible dreams. Give me the courage to start living them, the humility to start at the bottom and the patience to keep on.

STARTING SOMETHING NEW

O GOD, we are about to start something new. We believe that it is what you would like us to do. In our most confident moments we think that we can do it well. But sometimes we are not so sure.

You know the risks, God, and you know our weaknesses and our strengths. Keep us from confusion. Guard us from either pride or fear. Keep our hearts and minds open to you and to each other.

May we know the happiness of working together for you and the quiet joy of doing our best.

Happiness

SOMETIMES happiness comes, unsought, unexpected and unearned. All around me life is bright. I love you, I love people, I even love myself. Work is play, and peace and joy dance together.

Help me then, God, to use this blessing well. To share it and not keep it to myself.

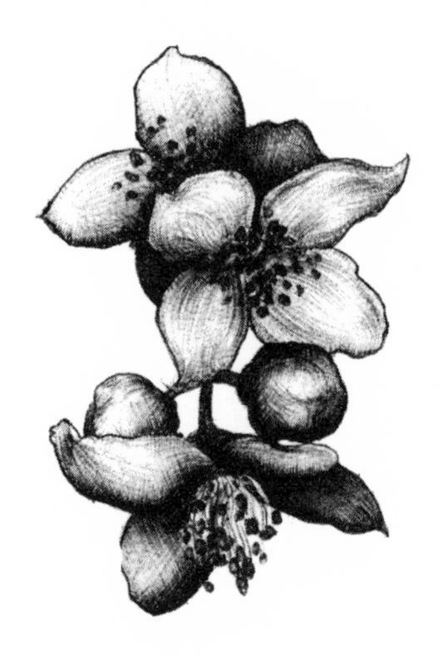

ON THE USE OF TALENTS

O GOD, help me to use the brains that you have given me without pride, the hands that you have given me without sloth and the tongue you have given me without malice.

For prisoners

GOD, if sometimes I cannot do as I want and it makes me angry, help me to remember the thousands in prisons who can seldom do what they want, who are miserable and afraid and far away from home.

O God, let them know you and give them comfort, hope and freedom once again.

To be patient with my mother and father

God, sometimes it is easier to love people who are not as close to you as your parents. I expect my mother and father to be perfect, and I get angry and hurt when they are not. I depend on them when I should be independent, and I rebel when I should listen. And sometimes I just close them out because I don't know what else to do.

Help me, God, to understand and accept them as they are. And help them to accept me.

LOVING OUR NEIGHBOR

JESUS, you know what it is to be human and that it is not easy to love our neighbor as ourselves.

When we do not understand our neighbors, nor they us, help us to think more about how we could understand them and less about how they could understand us.
May we never let fear keep us from speaking or acting in love, nor thoughtlessness spoil the impulse of the heart.

May we do all that we do in gratitude to you, rather than in desire for praise, and when our time, energy or talent are at an end, may we quietly ask your help and remember that you love and care for them much more than we do.

A SIMPLER LIFE

LIFE has gotten confusing, complex and full of pressures, God. I am pulled this way and that by too many demands and desires.

It is impossible to be my best self in the midst of this. Yet it is also hard to know how to make life simpler.

Help me to choose, God. Everything I do seems like something I *should* do, and yet I know that if I do not stop doing some things I will be able to do nothing well.

And if I do not leave some peace and quiet to listen to you, I will fail you, myself and others.

For someone very sick

GOD, someone I love is very sick. He is in pain and I cannot help. He may even die, and I am afraid.

O Father, you who made us all, take away his pain and make him well!

And renew both his spirit and mine so that we may better love and serve you.

CREATION

GOD, sometimes I hold something small in my hand, a piece of moss or a budding twig, and, peering closely at this tiny world, I feel a sudden wonder.

Help me to remember that you made these worlds and countless others and, in remembering, come closer to you.

For leaders

O God, help our leaders to lead. Whether they are ordinary people whom everyone copies or the heads of organizations or countries, help them to use their power well.

Don't let them get so proud they forget what they are doing or so busy that they forget you. Fill them with so much love that they can understand their followers and make peace with their enemies.

TEACH US THE WAYS OF PEACE

CHRIST, no one on earth really wants the pain and horror of war. We do not want to kill or to be killed, to hurt or to be hurt. But we all see injustice, and sometimes it makes us very angry and we see no other way to right the wrong except by war. Yet we know that a new great war may destroy us all.

We feel small and helpless.

Christ, teach us the ways of peace! Calm our angry hearts and grant to all peoples and their leaders unending patience in the search for peace and justice. Teach us and all men to be ready to give up some of our comforts and power and pride so that war will leave the face of the earth and we may work for you in peace.

SOMEONE HAVING TROUBLE

O JESUS, if I see someone having trouble, help me to stop instead of walking by. Help me to feel his trouble as if it were my own.

Tell me what to say or do to make it right and to feel love for him in his trouble, when he most needs love.

The exam

O Lord, perhaps I haven't used my eyes, my ears or my mind the way you would have me, but in any case, now it is too late. I know I can't ask you to put facts in my head I should have had there long ago, but, Lord, help me not to forget what I have learned and not to be so tense that I do not do my best.

And when this exam is over, help me to use all my chances to learn and not waste them.

WHEN SOMEONE HAS DIED

O CHRIST, someone whom I loved very much has died and there is an empty place I cannot fill. My heart aches and inside I feel stiff and tired. Help me, Christ, to look straight at that empty place and not be frightened. Help me to be glad for him because he is happy with you. And, O God, help me to be unafraid to walk the earth without him but to take strength and comfort from your love.

Bewildered

O Lord, when I am bewildered and the world is all noise and confusion around me and I don't know which way to go and am frightened, then be with me. Put your hand on my shoulder and let your strength invade my weakness and your light burn the mist from my mind. Help me to step forward with faith in the way I should go.

To be thankful

I **HAVE** many things to be thankful for, God, and sometimes I remember them and other times I forget. When something large or small goes wrong, it fills my mind and I forget those things for which—when I remember—I am thankful.

Help me to remember the good things, God. To name them, to savor them and to be thankful to you.

WHEN ANGRY WITH A FRIEND

O FATHER, I am very angry with my friend and I don't want to be. Help me to calm my anger before I say or do the wrong thing. Show me why he acted the way he did and help me understand him.

If I did something wrong, help me to know it and say I'm sorry. If I did nothing wrong, help me to be patient and forgive him.

AT THE END OF A BAD DAY

O FATHER, I hurt inside tonight. Nothing has gone the way it should. I didn't do very well and people thought I did worse than I did. Take the tiredness away from me, God; make me feel all in one piece again. Show me what I should do to make things better. Then let your peace descend on my heart so I can sleep well and get up tomorrow with your happiness upon me and ready to do better.

Little things

Lord, help me with little things that I forget. Remind me of the compliment that I should give, the letter to the friend I miss, the kind word I meant to speak to someone sad.

And when there are little things I want to do but shouldn't, hold me back. Help me to stop the cutting word, the boast, the scorn, the unkind laugh.

In all these things, O Lord, help me to remember always how the other person feels and to act in love toward him.

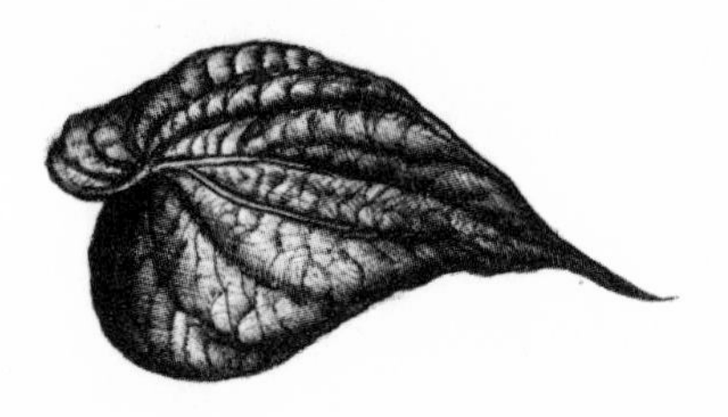

Friendship

O God, I thank you for my friends and all the joys that they have brought. I thank you for the happiness of sharing work and problems and laughter and for the joy of adventuring and learning together. I thank you for the chance to love and be loved, not because of cleverness or goodness but in spite of faults and differences.

Doubt

O God, when all the world looks gray and dirt shows everywhere and nothing is as it should be, I wonder if you really are.

O God, help me when I feel like this: Help me to remember the days when you were near and I knew it. Even when you seem far away, help me never to turn my back on you. Set me on the path to you and help me hold fast through the night, until I find your light once more.

For the Hungry and Hopeless

O Lord, in many places that I seldom or never see there are people hungry and without hope. Sometimes because I am not near them I forget and because I have not felt their troubles they don't seem real. But when I stop and dare to think, I know that they are real.

Lord, help these people whom I do not know and help me to help them. Give them strength and hope and take away their despair.

For those in pain

O God, when I in happy health can run and breathe and sleep without thinking it might be otherwise, do not let me forget those for whom each step is a fight with pain.

O God, help them! Make the unbearable bearable, and soften the constant hurt. Give them hope for the future, courage for the present and comfort from knowing you.

God's Workers

O God, help those whose whole lives are given to helping people find you.

Help those who are priests and ministers to love you and your Church. Help those who preach to speak from the heart as well as the head—and the head as well as the heart.

Grant wisdom, courage and love to those who must speak to people who are sick or in trouble. Help those who have dull jobs to find joy and meaning in their work.

Give teachers understanding of what they are teaching, and how to teach it. Help those who must be in charge of many people not to lose sight of you because they have too much to do.

Give them all a dream of what they might do and your love and patience to do it.

I AM NOT ALONE

I **AM** alone but not alone, and I am grateful. Not only are you with me, God, but so, in spirit, are all that great company of people who try to follow you.

Even living near me there are people I don't know who love you as I love you. Every time I try and fail and am forgiven and try again, I feel the unseen companionship of many other people.

You have a family, God, a family millions strong and yet still close. It gives me strength and comfort to remember this, and I thank you.

A GRACE

FATHER, we thank you for this meal, for our lives, for other people, for beautiful things, for goodness and for you.

A DEPARTURE

GOD, someone we love is leaving today and we will miss him. Keep him safe while he is gone. May the people that he meets add to his life and he to theirs. Whether in work or play, in safety or danger, on new paths or old, stay with him wherever he goes and whatever he does.

A BLESSING

O LORD, bless all the people I love, at home and far away. Guide them by night and by day and keep them always under your loving care.

And, O Lord, bless too the people I don't love as I should. Teach me to understand them and love them in spite of their faults. Help me to forgive those who act badly toward me and especially bless them as they need my love and yours.

To be old

To be old is to be the same but different. It is frightening, God, yet peaceful.

Death is closer and so are you. What is done is done and cannot be undone. Life lives on, day by day, but most of it is over.

How to make these last days count, God? To live them with courage, with little complaint. To give and receive small joys. To teach the best already learned and to learn yet a little more.

Nearer to you, we are more helpless. Without you, more lonely for you.

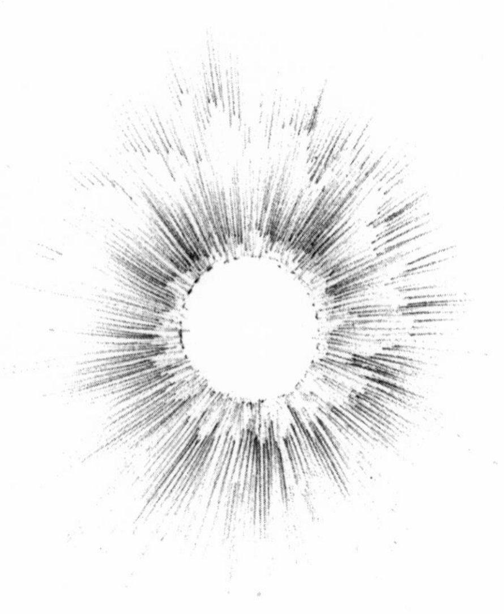

FOR TEACHERS

LORD, I pray for teachers:

Comfort them when they are misunderstood. Strengthen them when they must work under difficult conditions. Refresh them when their hours are long.

Above all, Lord, help them to give their pupils an infectious love of learning, work and excellence.

LEARNING

GOD, sometimes it is exciting to learn new things, and I thank you for the chance.

But there are other times when learning seems to be just dull and endless work. Help me then, God. Teach me how to concentrate and to be patient. Remind me of the good feeling of a hard job well done and of the new possibilities ahead when I have finished with the work I must do first.

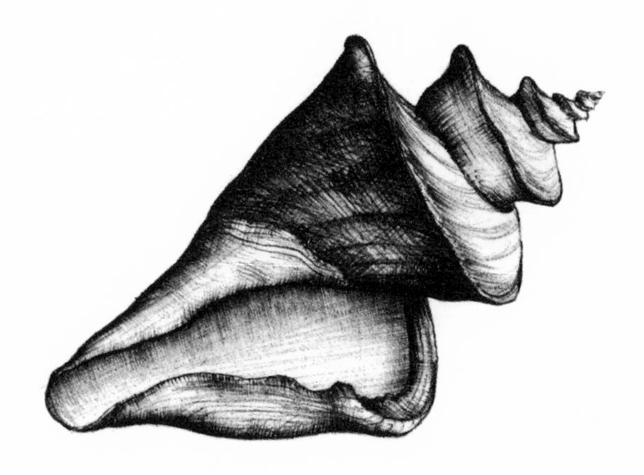

SELF-CONSCIOUSNESS

WHY can't I forget myself, God? I feel clumsy, awkward and stupid. And the more I feel that way, the more I am that way.

Help me to relax, God, and just be. And then, perhaps, I will be a bit nearer to the person you had in mind when you created me.

To see a lot of people

O God, I'm going to see a lot of people and I'm afraid I'll be wearing the wrong clothes, say the wrong thing and act the wrong way. I'm afraid no one will like me, and way down deep I'm afraid someone will laugh at me.

Help me, God. Take away my fear. I know it is stupid and still I'm afraid. Help me to know that other people are really afraid too and that behind smiling faces they feel cold and alone. Help me to want to soothe their fears and make them happy. Help me to think of them and forget myself.

PRIDE AND HUMILITY

I GET confused, God. When I can do something well it isn't the truth to say I do it poorly. And if someone tells me that *he* can't do something well, when I know he can, it irritates me.

Help me, God, to know when to speak and when not to. Remind me how I feel when I am not very good at something and others are. And guide my words so that they are truthful but not boastful.

WHEN I WANT TO DO SOMETHING WRONG

GOD, I want to do something I know is wrong. Please help me not to do it. Show me all the reasons why I shouldn't and give me strength to stand by them. Fill my heart with so much love for you that I want to please you more than I want to please myself.

THE IMPORTANT AND THE UNIMPORTANT

GOD, help me to see the difference between the important and the unimportant. Let nothing block my sight by seeming important when really unimportant or by seeming unimportant when really important.

AFRAID TO BE FOUND OUT

O LORD, I have done something wrong and I am afraid I will be found out. I am ashamed, but more than that, I am afraid that people who love me will be ashamed.

O Lord, I know it is my fault that I have done this thing and it cannot be undone but help me not to be a coward. If I ought to confess to someone, give me the courage. If I can make things better, show me how. And above all, do not let me add bad to bad because I am too afraid to let someone know what I have done.

Good yet quiet times

When I am full of joy or pain, it is easy to remember you, Lord, and to thank you or ask your help.

But there are some good yet quiet times when I never think of you. Times when work is hard but goes well, when friends are friends, when members of the family are together in quietness and love, when I have a chance to rest and be peaceful.

I thank you for these times, Lord. Help me to remember you then.

BROTHERHOOD

O FATHER, we know that deep inside us all is some part of you, for you made us all and we are all your children: in the person whose ways we don't like and the person who hates us, in the man as far away as our minds can think and the man so close our hands can touch. Everyone on earth is your child, and as we are all your children, so we are not strangers but brothers.

O God, help us to find you in ourselves and in everyone we meet and so learn to understand and love each other as you would have us.

GOD, MAKE ME WELL

O GOD, I have been sick a long time and almost forgotten how it feels to be well. The doctors do their best but they take a very long time. Help me to be as cheerful as I can so that my family are not too unhappy. And, O God, please make me well, so that my body can feel full of joy and I can run and shout and work and get tired and sleep and wake up happy.

As CHRISTMAS APPROACHES

CHRIST, forgive me for being so busy, confused and disorganized that I have little time to think of you as Christmas approaches.

Help me to pause, to think, to share, to listen, to learn so that I may better love you and all men in joyful gratitude for your birth.

A CHRISTMAS PRAYER

CHRIST, we want you to be born in us but we are unready. Change us with your light as you once changed the stable in Bethlehem.

Where our lives are too full to make room for you, help us to simplify them.
Where areas of our hearts and minds are shut tight against you, help us to open them.
Where we are too blind or proud to be penitent, help us to love you until your light reveals both our faults and your mercy.

Love and Practicality

Jesus, help us to remember your love while dealing with practicalities and help us to remember practicalities while caught up in loving you.

WHAT YOU WISH US TO DO

O GOD, open the eyes of our minds that we may see what you wish us to do and then give us the will, the courage, the intelligence and the love to do it.

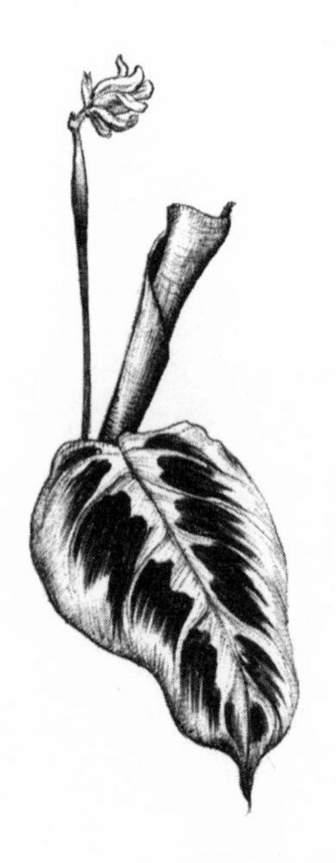

HELP US TO SEE

HELP us not to fool ourselves with words, God, with talk of being sorry when we are not sorry, with talk of sacrifice when we have no intention of sacrificing, with talk of action when we are too lazy to act.

Where our vision is dim, help us to see. Where our hearts are imprisoned by fears, release them. And when we see and feel your truth, give us the courage to act.

THE END OF THE WORLD

O GOD, help me to worry less about the end of the world, or the end of my life, or terrible things that may happen tomorrow, so that I may live to the full each moment of today.

WE HAVE BEEN WASTEFUL

CHRIST, we have been wasteful. We have loved ease and luxury and more to eat than is good for us. And now the world is running out of everything.

Forgive us, Lord, and teach us how to change our ways, to care for the earth you made and to learn how to give everyone what he needs.

AN EASTER PRAYER

CHRIST, we thank you for all rebirths. We thank you for forgiveness and for second chances, both for ourselves and others.

This Easter season as sleeping seeds and trees begin to burst into new life, help us all to become more alive and to grow more nearly into the people you mean us to be.

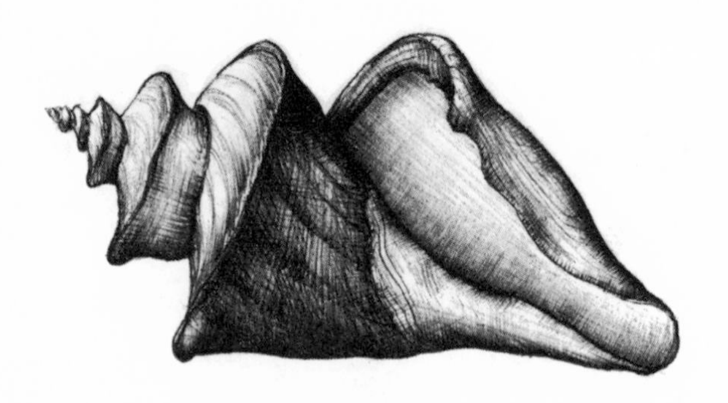

The troubles of others

God, help us to enter into the troubles of others, know them as if they were our own and act accordingly.

Small steps

God, help me to respond to your love for me more nearly as I should. Rouse me from inaction, from dreams I never try to bring to reality, from gratitude I feel but do nothing about.

I know that I am unable to do great things for you, God, but help me to be neither too lazy nor too proud to take such small steps as I am ready to take.

THE KINGDOM OF GOD

O FATHER, when everyone turns his back on you and thinks only of his own plans and not yours, when all is blackest, help us to know, more surely than day follows night, that your kingdom will come.

Help us to remember that deep inside all of us lies the living plan for your kingdom, ready to unfold and grow.

God, help us to search out this kingdom, to learn its ways and to call you king. Help us not just to hope for its coming but to work for it in thanksgiving and live it with joy.

YOUR WILL, NOT OURS

O FATHER no matter what we want or our friends want or our enemies want, may your will be done:

> Where we do not know you, help us to find you.
> Where we forget you, help us to remember you.
> Where we turn against you, bring us back to you.
> Where we fail you, forgive us and lead us once again where you would have us go.

OUR COUNTRY

O CHRIST, we love this land. We wish it were always a simple love and often it is, but life has become complicated. Good gets mixed up with evil and mountains of laws and regulations and numbers and systems get in our way when we wish to make everything work as it should. When things go wrong it becomes easy to give up, to blame other people and to do nothing.

O Christ, give us the unashamed courage to believe in the highest and the best ideals of our country, and enough passionate patience to make them come true.

HATE

JESUS, I am full of hate. I feel deeply hurt and unfairly treated. I am bitter and angry. I feel like hitting out, like sweeping someone from the face of the earth.

Jesus, you who know what human pain and hurt feel like, who felt men's hatred, ridicule and rejection. You who died at men's hands, deserted by your friends but still feeling and speaking love, root out my bitterness. Change my heart so that I may understand and love.

As you taught us

O **Christ**, as you taught us:

Help us not only to be fair but to be generous.
Help us not only not to fight but to make peace.
Help us not only not to steal but to give.
Help us not only not to lie but to search for the truth.
Help us not only not to do wrong but to do right.
Help us not only not to harm those who harm us but to forgive and help them.
Help us not only to love you but to serve you.

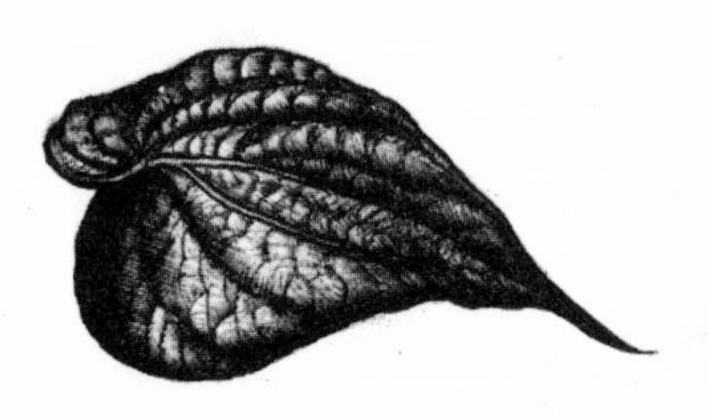

WHEN I HAVE LOST MYSELF

O GOD, I thank you for the place where no one goes but you and I; for the secret field, the tree, the rock, the corner in the house, where I may go and find myself again and, in finding me, find you.

What longed-for peace creeps in upon my heart, when, hidden in this secret place, I listen to the silence and slowly lose that tightness that held me fast, unhappy and afraid!

In time I find I can look around at your quiet things, the leaf so very near my head, the lines on the board beneath my feet or the bird that scolds a bit because I'm here and flies away. And when I've looked at those awhile and rested in the hush, I know that you are near and I can find myself again.

I AM WORRIED

O LORD, I am worried. I know that it does me no good to worry but I cannot shake it off.

It not only does no good to worry; it does harm. What I cannot change, I cannot change, but meanwhile, if I am this caught up in worry, I'm apt to do poorly what I could do well.

Help me to trust to you those concerns beyond my reach so that I may give my full attention to living each moment as it comes.

TO SEE YOU IN ALL THINGS

O CHRIST, help us to see you, not only in the big things of life where your action is clear, but in the little everyday things that come to hand. In these and in all things, may we find love and serve you.

FEAR

GOD, I am afraid. Not just of one thing but of many. It is not panic, just a quiet fear that has crept into places where I usually walk unafraid and is standing between me and people who wish me no harm.

There is good reason for some of the fear, God. But more of it is unreal. I know this and yet I cannot seem to throw it off. And whether real or imagined, it makes me less able to be myself.

Take this fear from me, God, that I may move freely in your world and be more nearly the person you wish me to be.

I MAY NOT GET WELL

ALWAYS, before this, I've just been sick for a while, a few days or a week or so. Once it was a matter of months. But now I realize that I may not get well. I may have to live with this pain until I die.

I don't want to face that, God. Neither pain that doesn't go away, nor death. I know that they come to us all, but I am not ready. Not anywhere near ready.

Help me, God. Give me the hope, the patience and the courage that I need. Help me not to be too envious of those who are well. Take away my anger and resentment so that I don't hurt those around me. Help me to use my reduced energies and opportunities to the best of my ability. And above all, give me greater love and understanding for my family, my friends and all those I see from day to day.

OUR GROWTH

O CHRIST, help us to grow:

In our knowledge of you,
In our knowledge of who you would have us be,
In our understanding of what your life means in our lives,
In our understanding of others,
In our commitment to growth in knowledge, understanding, love and obedience.

Mourning

He is gone; his pain is over and he is gone. The funeral is over and the family and friends have left. The letters are answered. But the emptiness remains.

The emptiness and so much more. I am *angry*, God. I am angry at him for dying and angry at you for letting him die. I am angry at friends, who have been so kind, because they are alive and because those they love are alive.

I am angry because I failed him so often. I hurt him. I was selfish, thoughtless, mean. And now he is gone, and I cannot undo the past.

It might be easier to pretend I am not angry but I cannot fool you, God. Help me through this time of anger and pain, of guilt and loss. Help me to live as he—and you—would like me to live.

A DIFFICULT DECISION

GOD, I don't know what to do.
Obviously whatever I decide, it will make a great difference. I have gathered all the information I need. I have weighed those things for and against. I have asked the advice of experts and friends. And I still don't know what to do.

Help me, God, to choose wisely. And once I have chosen, help me to go forward in faith.

WORK

GOD, a while ago my work seemed right to me. It gave me challenge and satisfaction and I was content.

But now it seems heavy and dull and long. I feel half alive when I work and surely this is not what you wish.

Help me to have the courage to change what is open to change and do what I must with lightness of heart.

Loneliness

I AM lonely, Christ. It hurts even to say it to you. I know that you are with me and that helps, but I need human companionship too.

Help me put my loneliness to good use. To turn to you more often. To reach out to others more than I usually do. To dare to share more of myself with others without fear of their misunderstanding or disapproval. Help me to remember that behind cheerful masks many other people are lonely and waiting for me, or someone, to befriend them just as I wait for them.

DISCOURAGED

O CHRIST, I am discouraged. I've worked and worked. I've tried new ways. I've thought about this problem till I've ached from weariness. I've discussed it with those who might help. And I don't know what to do next.

Christ, help me to see your will and your way and give me the strength to follow through.

AMEN

O FATHER, may everything that you are
become everything we want to be.
May everything that we have said to you in
love be remembered by us, now and always.

Index

FOR OTHER PEOPLE

EVERYDAY PRAYERS

BLESSINGS, GRACES AND THANKSGIVING

RELATIONSHIPS

DISCOURAGEMENT, SORROW AND CONFUSION

BEGINNINGS AND ENDINGS